More Than Flesh

Queen of Spades

Disclaimer

Some content in this book may not be suitable for all people. Reader's discretion is advised.

Table of Contents

Childhood for One

Is there a place where I can purchase
Childhood?
Is it at an obscure outlet mall or found
online?
Are the prices listed on the item final,
Or can we negotiate the nickels and
dimes?

Does this Childhood come attached
with a warranty:
A thirty, sixty, *even* ninety-day trial?
So I can arrange to have It fixed or
promptly returned
If none of Its elements make me smile.

Does this Childhood have Customer
Support
That I can have access to 24-7?
Is that an add-on; if so, can I get it for
free?
I've got many questions I want to ask
Heaven.

I want to ask ... why so much *adversity*?
Can't most of the lessons be taught
with *less* stress?
Why, way back then, I didn't have *true*
friends?
It may have helped with the strife, I
must confess.

Also, why was I launched into
dysfunction.
Where no one knew how to act
Or behaved in extremes?

Shutting down to where nothing is ever
talked about,
Or people being passive-aggressive,
cutthroat, and mean?

Yes, I'd like to purchase a Childhood!
I'm so sick of **never ever** feeling young
Like the little kids I've read about in my
books:
Smiling, playing, and having fun.

It's a *headache* being programmed for
Purpose,
Feeling the spiritual state of the World's
humanity,
Having a built-in, high-functioning
emotional radar
That senses hodgepodges of empathic
energy.

Can I get a Childhood *without* all that
extra?
I'll do Pay in 4 installments ... whatever
it takes!
Universe, I can't help but wonder
without all the "gifts",
Could a normal Childhood have been
great?

Lack of YOU

*One cannot love
One cannot miss
That was never there.*

Back then, I declared.

Currently,
I've been seeing threes,
So I've been slowly unpacking,
Re-examining what I was decreed.

She told me Your name,
But I don't know if it's true
That the other half of me
Is a reflection of You.

There's *no* mention of You
On any legal papers
Nor were there attempts by either party
To rectify this later.

Nonetheless,
Because You were *never* there,
It was easy to convince myself
That I never *cared*.

And ... because it was her
Who for a short time remained,
It was *convenient* placing the onus on
her
For feeling all the pain.

Misdirected
More like
Imbalanced

It would have been nice
If You were curious
About how I'm doing in life.

It would have been great
To have You vet any person
That I wanted to date.

It would have been cool
For You to have attended
All my events at school.

It would have made me smile
If I'd had a proper wedding
For you to walk me down the aisle.

*But these would haves
Never came to pass.*

The only man I knew as Daddy
Has been gone for a spell.

He stepped in without hesitation
And I think he did rather well.

It took his sudden departure
For what was buried to become dug up,
So for the *first time ever*, I confess
Your absence and indifference hurt.

I'm not expecting an apology.
I don't need an explanation
Or promises to do better and be
proactive.

Just do You.

Continue to Live.

I just wanted to lessen the burden
On how the lack of You impacted me,
So that the walls around my heart can
soften
And it can be open to forgive.

Wake Up, Daughter

I speak to one of the two seeds that
never came to be.
I cannot say if it was meant to be or
destiny.
I may feel more comfortable just stating
I waited too long,
But the more honest reason is the
person in question was wrong.

Dearest Kyra,

The daughter who never came to be
The one who would have facial features
That closely resembled me

First dressed in yellow and blue
I was never a fan of pink
I would read you a mixture of books:
Fiction and works to make you think.

I want to tell you what was never told
to me,
*For the ones before me didn't have the
capacity.*
Whether right or wrong, all did their
best,
But with these words, maybe you'll have
less stress.

Wake up, Daughter.

Your eyes have the power to soothe
souls.
Be selective in who you have around
you
So that won't be rendered cold.

Wake up, Daughter.

Enjoy your innocence and youth.
Don't be that woman aching with regret
Mourning over what cannot be
recouped.

Wake up, Daughter.

Make sure one's words and actions are
aligned.
The moment your intuition says danger,
Plan your escape; don't waste time.

Wake up, Daughter.

Be You — intentionally with no
apologies.
Never get fooled by any person
Wanting to dim You for coupledom to
succeed.

Wake up, Daughter.

Avoid all the missteps that I did before.
You'll appreciate and value life so much
more.
Although we never came together in
this life,
I'm confident in the next one,
We both turned out alright.

With everlasting love,
Mama

Don't Run, Son

I speak to one of the two seeds that
existed in another life.
To my dismay, his soul was polluted
with numerous moments of strife.
I may give myself comfort by saying *I
did the best I could*,
But how can one have a successful crop
where the soil is no good?

Dearest Michael,

The one who always felt out of place
Thought *nothing* came from being good
anyway

If I could rewind the hands of the clock,
I would have pursued this differently
By not choosing a boy in a man's shell
Lacking the tools to succeed.

In hindsight, I should have been fully
transparent
Instead of letting you believe I was the
bad parent.
I didn't want you seeing him in a
negative light
Although *despite* what you were told,
He was the one who took flight.

Don't run, Son.

Allow yourself to feel the pain.
Don't continue to numb and suppress.
It may lead to going insane.

Don't run, Son.

Don't rush to save everybody!
Because when your ass was in a sling,
Who was there for you?
NOBODY.

Don't run, Son.

Open your heart as well as your ears.
Don't gaslight, get roused to anger,
Or bolt at the words you don't want to
hear.

Don't run, Son.

My bond with your father: once pure,
became tainted,
But continuing the cycle *should not* be
your fate.
Seek out all of the methods to bring
forth healing.

Quit running, Son.

For You, it's NOT too late.

With restorative faith,
Mama

When They Seep Through

In the wee hours of early morn
Or while listening to a tune,
No one can predict
When they seep through.

While adding eggs to the cake batter
Or watching the spinning of a dryer,
It *never* seems to matter
When they seep through.

Conglomerations of unpleasantness
For years was conveniently cast away.
Valleys morphed into mountains,
Then its own woman-formed island.

But what can appear to be dormant
Is *often* lying in wait.
It only takes the right amount of
pressure
To open the floodgates.

In the middle of a meeting
Or while deciding what to wear,
No one can forecast
When they seep through.

While composing an email
Or picking out a fitness class,
Feet *cannot* run fast enough
When they seep through.

The containment of my emotions
Gave way to psychological implosion.
I mistook being in spiritual autotune
For orchestrating a perfect tune.

I had to remove that contact lens
From my third eye.

The covering was *blinding* me,
Not rehabbing me.

Because *scabbing over*
Doesn't mean the issues are over.
The scabs are cover-ups that delay
Recovering enough ...

Recovering enough to see
That *what* was done to me
Does NOT define me.

That I'm *More Than*

Afterthoughts when other possibles fell
through
Transactions when others were in
financial crises
Menstrual pads to absorb others' pain
and suffering

In the wee hours of the morn
Or while listening to a song,
I close my eyes, still breathing
While feeling them seep through.

While sitting on the bed,
Snapshots flashing in my head,
My body outwardly trembles
As they seep through.

The ocean of tears unshed
Crashed against what I created.
By letting them seep through,
The structures were decimated.

Looking out at the horizon
Imagining my life anew.
By plucking all the scars open,
Now healing can seep through.

Sage of the Heart

Hey there,
You know I'm tryin'.

Honestly, there's no denying
An unquantifiable dereliction
In my interpretation
Of what love looks like.

It's not outright disobedience,
Just a tussle within myself.

Mainsprings shoved into bottomless
boxes
Thrown in the attic, collecting cobwebs
Never to be discovered.

Whoever said,
"Never is a promise
That's guaranteed to unfold"
Underestimated the fortitude
Of spiritual zeal
To guide one to ascension.

So ... I cleared away the cobwebs,
Sliced through the ribbons of Duct tape,
Flung open the boxes
To unearth what my coping skills
Attempted to shield me from.

Aye, young so young!

Back then, ached to fit in.
Back then, desperately wanted friends.

I didn't have enough support
To guide me away from false narratives,
But I didn't have enough decibels
To make my voice audible.

Children should be seen
And not heard, right?

That is what I was taught
Was alright.

I was bullied for a stretch of time,
And it felt never-ending,
But it was around the early teens
When the teasing changed to touching.

The extra clumps of fat
On my chest
Was now providing

Fascination
Stimulation
Amazement

Curious as to whether
They were real

Visualization
Sexualization
Provocation

I lost count of how many times
The school bus was used as a cover
For all things unspoken.

All I wanted was to be *left alone*
On my ride home.

But as my baby fat got redistributed
To grown-looking titties and a matching
ass
Around age thirteen,
I was seen differently.

My innocence was

Poked at,
Prodded with,
Laughed at

And I didn't have the tools to know
That it was emotional malpractice,
Orchestrated to fuel their thirsty egos
And make me a member of their
depravity.

I got told that older guys
Feeling on my body
Was a rite of passage
And that it happened to *everybody*.

I got told that the guys
Making me stroke them off
Was a good thing.

It meant that I was

Beautiful
Sexy
Wanted

Right then, I was impregnated.
Rapidly birthed compartmentalization,
Fast-tracked the mastery of
multitasking.

Every day, appearing whole,
But strutting around segmented.

One-third of me perpetually
asphyxiated;
One-third of me suffered mental
inflammation via gaslighting;
One-third of me possessed with
ischemia of my intuition

The PhDs in separation in functionality
Set the tone for my sharps and flats in
love.
Yes, the choices were lackluster,
But it was all my Inner Child could think
of.

Yet Ascension demands

Authentication,
Identification,
To suss out the lies,
To unwaveringly say ...

To not be comfortable in your
femininity
Is NOT okay.

To be seen as a WOMAN when you're
still a child
Is a form of perversion.

To be touched and to force someone
To touch one's private parts
Is sexual assault.

To be told

"Boys will be boys."
"That's how they show love."
"That's how you fit in."
"That's a rite of passage."

Is psychological torment
And emotional rape.

They were not my friends.
They were not my tribe.
They did not have my best interests at
heart.
They watched while puberty tore me to
shards.

I have an extremely long road
Before I can truly see black men as safe.
Yet, I remain, exhuming these bones ...

Hey You,
Please see I'm tryin'.

Sandpaper

Inhale clean sheets
Exhale simple bliss
Fingers slid across the clothesline
When strong hands gripped my hips.

Should have stayed
To view Mother Nature on display

But Lust called
And I decided to answer.

Inhale my lover's scent
Exhale my burning desire
Panties ... the only item torn away
As those hands hoisted me higher.

Moaning *Like*
Saying *Lust*
Screaming *Fuck*

My body lowered upon climax
Whispered *Love* into my ear.
On the bed, we collapsed.

Inhale vanilla extract
Exhale simple pleasure
Eyes observing mixing of the cake
batter
Predicting tastiness beyond measure.

Should have stayed
To confirm the dessert's perfection

But the soft lips on my neck
And the manicured nail grazing my
breast
Skewed my mind's direction.

Inhale my lover's perfume
Exhale my proscription
My apron and other clothing
Met the floor of the kitchen.

Moaning *Love*
Saying *Love*
Spelling

Y

E

S

Next to my sinful swell

And as we reached our peaks,
You swore to *everyone* it was *Kismet.*
So much so that I believed.

Observe soiled sheets
Exhalation staggers
Hand cupping a once treasured cove:
Pounded, bruised, battered.

Whatever happened to the days
Before Reality entered my world
And the falseness of You remained?

Now those strong hands
Are made for

Pulling
Pushing
Waving

... goodbye

Moving on to the next person
To stroke Your Ego.

For the little *Love* that was whispered
Was the first to go,
Followed closely by *Like.*

Soon, along came *Lust*,
Finding Its home inside another.

Observe packed boxes
Exhalation ceases
Hands clutching at my chest
As if to hold tight the pieces.

Whatever happened to the nights
Before the truth of You came to bloom
When You filled my days with
Affirmations
And my nights with Physical Touch?

Kismet must have said,

I'll
Do
You
With
A
Rusty
Blade

Because I got sliced
On all sides.

The highs of your insatiable mania
The depths of your heightened
depression
The unorthodox methods of emotional
release

Left the immaculate state of my skin
deceased,
Sank its teeth and drained me of my
zest
Until I had no clue how to

Provide
Satiate
Satisfy

Anyone *except* You.

... but that wasn't enough
And You *left* anyway.

Inhale incense
Exhale slowly
Reminiscing over who I believed were
Soul mates
But fizzled into examples of Soul *fakes*.

Observe Freedom
Exhale Peace

I recognize pain is the compass for learning
But want the magnitude of such to cease.

Hangup

Leaving lines on "read"
Knowing that it's been a while.
In most situations, it's an individual
Who messaged back or dialed.

Yeah, I've never been like most
And through the years,
I've been told

It's a bad thing;
It's a sad thing;
It's a hangup

And that I'm messed up.

When demons can't penetrate the
heart,
They often go for the mind.
Wounds laced with misdirection and
deception
Makes truth and reality really hard to
find.

Can you really expect from me clarity
When the lenses are full of scratches?
Am I really being cruel or just protecting
myself
When I often engage in detachment?

Staring at these crafted walls
For what seems an eternity.
In most affairs, an object is kept
When it's serving someone's needs.

... but this atypical affair is an
awakening,
And most recently, Spirit said to me:

The wall is an illusion.
The wall is an obtrusion:
A cluster of monstrosities
To be demolished with expediency.

It's a good thing.
It's a sure thing,
But it'll get others hung up.

It's an inception
Of infinite directions,
Leading to what I recognized all
along—
This is how I'm made up.

More Than a Secret

Is it a superpower
To talk yourself out of the feels
To see the sensibility of all sides?

At the juncture of re-examining

If the feels were real
If the outrage was just
If I over-romanticized our connection

If there ever was an Us?

Shiiiit, overthinking must be the Devil,
For my heart knows the truth.

You're out there living your life,
Building and achieving with your new
beau,
Claiming it was only a phase
And it's what "curious": ones do.

When *You* know
And I know
That our deal
Wasn't fragments
Or figments
Of imagination.

That we largely had in common
Sisterhood experiences
And college goals.

You cannot fix your lips
To mouth those words
That our chit chat
Wasn't swollen
With innuendos
That would make nuns blush.

I *know* when eyes look *beyond*
And crawl inside
Because that was the transaction
Between You and me.

Tearing down the "just friends" wall
Was an inevitability.

But You got spooked:
Became scared
Became unsure

Muddied what I classified
As satiating
Sacred
Unique

Took the treasure
I swore I found in Us
And tossed it like trash.

You treated me like some splurge
purchase
That You changed your mind about ...

Like I was never there.

*Ooooh, I've got to shake this Devil
loose!*

Even in my duplicity,
My heart knows the truth.

Your fear of backlash
Doesn't erase the fact
That we arched each other's backs.

Your battle with whether
It was right or wrong
Doesn't negate

The emails,
The phone calls,
Or the visits.

Your indecision
With what to do with me
Doesn't contradict
That You *toyed* with me.

My understanding
Why you were unfaithful
Doesn't dull the jolt
You served my heart.

Although another was convinced
He secured the title,
My very first love
Was actually **You**.

The lamella crusting on my heart
Started in high school,
But the incision of hardening
Blossomed with You.

You, more than likely,
Will never read this
Nor will we ever again meet.

Yet, the question lingers:
**Will I reach the echelon
Of this emotion again?**

All the Universe says is,
"We shall see."

Bag Lady

The sturdy
Brown paper bag
With purpose

Gosh, so many memories!

I'd divide the paper bag
Then shape it
So it'd cover my favorite book
Perfectly.

I would use crayons and colored pencils
To illustrate my own design,
So that no matter what else transpired,
I'd look upon it

And believe all was fine.

The sturdy brown paper bag faded
With the hype about plastic ones.
Not a creative sit-in like its predecessor
But still got some stuff done.

One could utilize the handles
To keep the contents steady.
It was easier to double and triple layer
it
When I wanted to pack it heavy.

Packing plastic bags with weight
Became a skill I did best,
Realizing few and far between ever
appeared
To lift any mass from my chest.

Eventually, due to overpacking,
Or being recycled in excess,
The plastic bags ended up with holes,
So I tossed the entire mess.

The Hefty bags were the next logical
step:
Midnight black, extremely tough.
I could still push in all of my baggage,
But my body proceeded to slump.

Soon after, I could not determine
What kept my overall stature bowed:
The extra weight clinging to my frame
Or the bags I refused to put down.

Whatever the case, this necessitated a
break.
That's when I decided to minimize,
Not just changes in outward
appearance
But the contents I was hauling inside.

I no longer needed Hefty bags.
It's shocking how much stuff I had!
I just need a recycled sack every now
and again.
Current Soul status: feeling Glad.

Skin Tells the Story

I may not look like what I've been
through
But when all of my clothes come off,
My skin tells the story.

Like that oval on my right foot

I was handling a boiling pot.
The water unexpectedly splashed.
That spot was the aftermath.

And the scrape on my right knee

I was relatively young.
I ran too fast in my burgundy shoes,
Slid on the gravel road.
Knee bloody;
Ego bruised.

I may not reflect what I've survived
But when I disrobe to shower at night,
My skin tells the story.

Like that angled discoloration
On my right thigh

I can't recall what the hell
We fought about that night.

Only the **knife**

... it wasn't the last moment
The knife came into play.

I walked in on my companion
Putting blade to one's wrist.

I freaked out,
Not knowing this was
One's method of self-coping.

In the tussle,
The weapon cut deep.

On my left arm,
Just past the wrist.

That skin may have been saved
If that madness didn't exist.

I may not look like I've gone through changes
But when I'm standing nude in the mirror,
My skin tells the story.

The increase of light stretch marks
With *weight fluctuations*

The decrease in moisture retention
With *permutating hormones*

The difference in *texture*
Covering fat versus muscle

The effects on my breasts
With *decreased elasticity*

I know I'm not
In my twenties anymore,
But I appear shades better
Than some who come through the door.

Yeah, my skin tells many stories,
But I still feel tremendous glory.

Arith-ME-tic

It took subtracting from Religion
To add abundance to my Spirit.
I had to divide what was taught to me
In order to multiply my learning.

No matter what representation
I've *shown out* since birth,
Even before manifestation
When I was a mere suggestion
During the act of youthful coition.

Elimination at my genesis
Was never part of the blueprint.

It's like Spirit already knew
I had a whole lot to do.

It took subtracting from Belonging
To add vivacity to my Light.
I had to divide from the body of
Groupthink
In order to multiply the enhancement of
Soul Speak.

"All my life I had to fight"
Was more than some quoted line.

It was my staple, the day-to-day.
Bleaching the grime of every
misconception
That was splattered my way.

Signaling for defeat or retreat
Was never part of my bloodline.

I was fine.
I *will be* fine.
I. AM. FINE.

It took subtracting from unrealistic
visuals
To add appreciation for my Uniqueness.
I had to divide what I was told about my
body
In order to multiply my Acceptance of
its truth.

"Got a cute face for a big girl"
Is not a compliment.
It's a political way to sugarcoat
What is really meant.

Cue translation.

A woman isn't as attractive
When she has extra mass.
She's only suitable for desperate
dusties
Or a vestibule for easy ass.

I am that woman, who in the past,
Wouldn't receive a second glance.

Fast forward.

Now, I'm getting private messages
Citing remorse
Bestowing Compliments
And wanting another chance.

Sadly, I get more stimulation from my
leg day
Than any love bombing they spit my
way.

I get more thrills with gym machines
and free weights
Than tired traditional ideas of a great
first date.

Perhaps

One set of ten lines I have not heard
before
One set of twelve times I'm not called a
pet name
One set of fifteen times we've
conversed via phone

And I *may* consider
A pause in my fitness routine
... *or* just join me.

But I digress.

Seriously though ...

I've been *too aware* of this superficiality
And I've been *too bored* with
Humanity's mediocrity.

Therefore, if Humanity isn't committed
In the pursuit of elevating,
Then I'll take on the journey myself.
I've never been one for waiting.

Out of Sync

For Kangaroo

Hey You,
This is probably way overdue.

I wasn't holding on
To any resentment.

I was just processing,
Biding time,
Trying to pinpoint
When it was right
To say this to you.

Chile,
Soul Speak doesn't give a damn
About Humanity's time clock.

We've always stepped in rhythm:
Side-by-side or one following closely
behind.

... just lately, the pacing's been *strange.*

One of us is sprinting
While the other's stuck.

Yeah, I remember to look back.
Yeah, I come back for You.

In the interim, it didn't feel heavy.
It's what people who love each other
do.

Transcendence unmatched
When our minds are combined.

You: optimistic, always looking long
distance.
Me: pragmatic, peering in proximity.

... just lately, the fuel's been *suboptimal.*
Watered down by the stress of every
day.

I'm attempting the essence of You—
A role I'm not used to.
You are mired in Negativity ...
It's sad and *strange.*

To say I want things to revert
To the way they once were
Wouldn't be entirely true.

I remember the *roots* of Us:
Bodies riddled with trauma
Hearts heavy with sadness
Spirits worn.

It's *not* going in different directions
That has prompted this chat.
Changing over the years was inevitable:
An unspoken, absolute fact.

... just lately, it's starting to feel *heavy*.

How can my Soul remain light
When I feel my Twin Soul's light
Go dim, shrouded in darkness?

Know that the strength of Us never
relied
On how much we've been able to
survive.
We bonded in ways that showcased our
best.
That was the predecessor to the rest.

That's the goal: being our optimal
selves,
Traveling the path of healing together.

I say this from a place
Of awareness and concern
For You are a member of my tribe
And I'd like You to remain forever.

Let Me Explain

Way back when,
I've stated that I am
Hard to love.

Jumping to the present,
Not much has changed.

To be clear,
I have not transformed
Into the stereotypical

Angry black woman
Who
Doesn't need
Anyone
For shit

Nah, that ain't it.

Nor have I become

Broken
Bitter
And
Disillusioned

On the contrary

This singledom of my choosing
Was the preparation
Of the fortification—
The tears of my psyche
That required reparation
And rejuvenation.

Who knew that it took
Treasuring my *aloneness*
To make me a better candidate
If and when I choose to date?

Yet, I am *still*
Hard to love.

Because to love me
Exemplifies levels of *mental expansion*
That one may not be ready for.

Because to love me
Signals willingness of *emotional
maturity*
That may have one running for the door.

Because to love me
Represents *accepting truths* about my
identity
That one may not be able to
comprehend.

Because to love me
Acknowledges *compliance* with my
boundaries
Or without hesitation, seeing "Us" come
to an end.

Whether my *awakening* attracts others
Or has them fleeing for the hills,
The next potential loving connection
Will be of my own free will.

Heart Expansion

Over the years, I've meticulously crafted
My own by-laws of pragmatism,
And usually, layers of optimism
Couldn't squeeze through the concrete.

Notwithstanding

Putting in the work
And *manifesting* what works
Made me open a piece once sealed
To imagine what could be.

Spirit revealed years back
Someone was out there for me,
But I wasn't quite sure what to believe
Because those who appeared failed
miserably.

Love isn't half-assed.
Love isn't restrained.
Love isn't parceled in baggies
Only to open on a whim.

My heart short-circuited Love
Because of the story *I* told myself
When I went *all-in*
Although it boiled down
To the wrong receptacle.

No matter who came along,
That book stayed at my bedside.

When any wrong was done,
I could quote the very page
Of a similar crime,
And tell my heart, "See there.
This Love stuff ain't for us."

I was the one who had to shift
Tap into the reality
That I wasn't genuinely ready.

In order to get there,
I couldn't race like the hare
But more like the tortoise:
Slow and steady.

When my cup finally resumes
To healthily runneth over with Love,
Who was meant for me
Will be healthy enough to receive.

Soulgasm

My *body* is too shallow for the depth I
contain.

Maybe it's why, more often than not,
That my passion feels imprisoned.

My *heart* only holds a fraction of a
fraction
Of the galaxies of infinite intensities
Of immeasurable love I have to give.

My *brain* is too frigid for my *mind's*
flexibility.

I fear that is why oftentimes,
My thoughts are lost in translation.

My *soul* grows bored with interpersonal
interactions,
So in my attempt to pacify the void,
It partakes in sensations.

Those vices that would leave
A commoner confused.

Those phrases deemed by religious
zealots
As deviant incantations.

For who am I to claim
That my ecstatic cries of pleasure
Are truly in Spirit's name?

What *I* do know
In this *time*
In this *life*.

No matter whether I was

A brief friend with benefits
A long-time girlfriend
Or a devoted dutiful wife

There's not been *one human*

To empty the fuel of an overthinking
mind
To improve my knowledge with a word
spoken
To keep the vivacity of love overfloweth
To mindfully ensure my heart wasn't
broken

There was no clear superior
In regard to gender.
Neither side was ever successful
In obtaining a surrender ...

One that rendered coming together so sublime
That I didn't regret leaving Singledom behind.

It's *only* when Spirit whispers to me
That I experience a shiver
Throughout my body.

It's *only* when Spirit touches me
That what was deemed dormant
Automatically rises.

There are

No hands
No lips
No tongue
No pole

That can compete with the way
Spirit makes me unfold.

Retiring My Sidekick

It's awkward for me
To say this out loud,
But maybe there are people
Who can relate to this.

After having been coupled
Now currently in Singledom,
The search for finding who's next
Does something funny to my chest.

Nope, it's not like "Ha-ha-ha".
Yeah, it's more like "Hell no"!

I can't tell if its indigestion or
palpitations
When my Inner Child starts running the
show.

All those potential red flags?

Red ain't nothin' but a hue.
He's always texting compliments
Although the quantity of contact is few.

Why doesn't he want to chat on the
phone?

Duh, obviously, he's a busy man.
You just have to be more patient.
He likes a woman who understands.

There are no discussions about our
meeting.
When there are, it's nothing concrete.

Girl, you must be more understanding
On what's going on in these streets.

When he finally wants a face-to-face,
It's always suddenly or on a whim.
He's never taking into consideration
On what activities I have taking place.

Look, if you want to make connections,
It all invoices sacrifice.
If you claim to be unavailable,
The opportunity may not come around
twice!

Inner Child, I'm sorry
You had to take what You could get.
I've become a more multifaceted adult.
In other words, I'm not desperate.

Inner Child, I'm sorry Life forced You
To constantly people-please.
I operated for a while, doing it Your
way,
But everyone was pleased except me.

Inner Child, I thank You
For just acting on what You deemed
was best,
But when it comes to dating in this
modern world,
I've got this handled; go get You some
rest.

The Algorithm Reject

I'm aware it's my Old Soul speaking,
But the days before Social Media
Were more authentic.

None of this *hiding* behind a computer screen
To say what you really mean.

None of this *manufacturing* a false life
For comments, retweets, and likes.

*That's what books and TV shows are
for, right?*

Anyway ...

There was also none of this rhetoric
About being hashtag worthy
Or trending for the algorithm.

But ... according to the algorithm,
We don't care about depth
Unless it can be conveyed
In ten minutes or less.

We aren't invested in doing the work
Unless the work is flashed on a screen
As easy-to-follow bullet points
On Tik Tok.

We're invested in drama.

Plucking out trigger words,
Acting like we're the "new woke"
Without delving into the context.

We're driven by division.

Arguing instead of listening,
Clapping back instead of considering
The other person's point of view.

What can I say?
I don't operate in this way.

I don't need to activate the algorithm
To let the world know
My existence has meaning.

To be frank, I value my peace
And don't engage in senseless
bickering.

I am in the business of Living life
Not creating an alternate life
To pander to an audience.

However ...

If that's how you get coins, do you.

If that's *not* you, just know
The viciousness of Social Media
If you ever fall out of the algorithm's
favor
Is *not* worth it in the end.

No cap—most of these followers
Are *trolls* and *fans*, not friends.

Also no cap, ya'll can have that.

The people who care enough about me
Know exactly where I'll be.
... and it's not constantly cruising Social
Media,
Riding these Internet streets.

Expounding: Affirmations

Affirmations without belief are whispers
Like ligules floating into the sky.
Yes, they are aware they are free
But have no destination.
No investment in the why.

Affirmations without origin are fleeting
Like catchy challenges or temporary
trends.
Yes, for a while, it can potentially make
do,
But like all that is just seasonal,
They come to an end.

Affirmations without motivation are
subjective
Depending on which vibe is taking the
lead.
Sure, proving the doubters wrong is
high octane fuel,

But not switching to energy that's more
sustainable
Will cause detours for healing to
succeed.

Affirmations are not statements done
on the fly
That one can whip up for others to
cosign.

Affirmations are beliefs that one
manifests
Performing actions to ensure one's
personal best.

Affirmations serve as reminders that
when one strays
That unlearning toxicity will get one
back on her way.

One doesn't have to spend thousands
On a spiritual retreat.

Unless one needed it anyway.

One doesn't even have to stockpile
Numerous self-help books.

Unless it's one's process to progress.

To give covenant of oneself
An everyday guiding voice,
The primary motivator
Simply boils down to choice.

True Fitness

Getting physically fit
Has absolutely no value
If toxic components of your Spirit
Are morbidly obese.

My therapist's tagline
Also known as
Catchphrase

Okay, let's unpack.

Most people from the past
I don't deal with anymore.

Guess you can say
I'm on a permanent fast.

I had too many transitional people
Putting fat deposits in my arteries,
Bringing forth high systolic and diastolic
numbers
Along with emotional Type 2 diabetes.

There were also too many fans
Cheering me on to my detriment.
Like granulated sugar, I put them to
pasture
Replaced with those caring about my
betterment.

At first, there were some cravings
And some resistance to the newness,
So a few stragglers nostalgically
reappeared,
Apprehending my steady progress.

Luckily, the present-day ritual
Eventually became my preferred
groove.
I was able to exorcise those remnants
And place them permanently on the
move.

Fitness is not just something
That's passe or a phase.
It's a compact to ongoing improvement
That I practice every day.

For it is when I'm physically,
Mentally,
Emotionally,
And Spiritually in sync
That I feel unmeasured euphoria
And infinitely complete.

Crystal Mesh

To get on my radar

Be bold with your game.
Ask about my thoughts and feelings,
Throw in some compliments.

Don't be an undercover mutha

Hittin' me up when you're bored
With "hey", "wyd", and "what's good"
Because that's just suspect and lame.

My Soul Complement should be like
Obsidian
Because I have moments when I take
flight.
Know when and how to communicate
effectively.
It's more about peace than being right.

My Soul Complement should show up
like Jade
In times when I'm crestfallen or blue.

Be the solution, or at least the listening
ear,
Instead of the source of the pain I've
gone through.

My Soul Complement should pop up
like Agate.
The type of hue: preferably yellow.
Showing up on the rare occasion
When I get anxious and do not feel
mellow.

My Soul Complement should radiate
like Turquoise.
Along the way, I do make mistakes.
Just know that my intent is not
malicious
And the best way to heal is by showing
grace.

My Soul Complement should embody
Sunstone
When energy is not where it needs to
be.
That special person can possess the
right magic
To place all elements in symmetry.

The only other ingredients to my Soul
Complement:
Rose Quartz mixed with Amethyst.
I could believe that individual is out
there
Or become my own Alchemist.

More Than Flesh

I peel away the urge to sacrifice
Just to make another satisfied.

I defy hanging all my traits in a closet
To pick and choose what is pleasing

To you
And you
... yes, even you!

I scoff at the obsession to characterize
Shoving who I am in one tidy box.

I gag at those who "claim" to know me now
When *my now* isn't the same
As *ten seconds ago.*

"Knowing is half the battle,"
Said G.I. Joe.

Some say I'm mysterious;
Some say I'm a handful;
Some say I'm the one who got away,
But I think I have them fooled.

For the next ones that come along
And vie for my attention,
You're chasing after more than you
bargained for.
I'm a whole 'nother dimension!

Know that when you're dealing with me,
You're getting a Trifecta.
All are going to shine at the same
speed.

If you ask me to dumb everything down
Because you can't comprehend what I
say,
I'm certainly not the person that you
need.

My Mind's not interested in the
foreskin;
It cuts deep.

What gets unraveled
Is not for the closeminded
Or the weak.

My Heart's not invested in frilly clichés;
It goes hard.
The intensity of emotions
Flows one of two ways:
Fire when filled with love
Ice when a lover departs.

My Spirit gives not one iota about flesh.
It detaches and sees beyond.
It's hard to possess the depth of an
ocean
When others' grasps are shallow ponds.

So ... for those who want to be "my
Last",
I encourage you to do and be your best.
Just know this isn't my first appearance
here,
For I am ... **More Than Flesh**.

Acknowledgments

It would be remiss of me to conclude this collection without thanking the following:

First and foremost, the Creator, who has blessed me with many gifts. I do not take those for granted and plan on utilizing them all.

Secondly, All Authors Publishing House, for their assistance in the creative process and execution. Also, FIG Publishing group for their support, as well as others in the writing community.

I also thank the ghosts of my past. Your haunting has provided me lessons to carry with me in the present and the future.

To my therapist Michelle, thank you for encouraging me to "unpack, examine, and process."

Last, and certainly not least, to those who have remained before, during, and after—You are truly my Tribe.

Author Bio

The best way to describe Queen of Spades is an Antiquated Hybrid: a contemporary author whose writings have a down-to-earth resonance to anyone who reads them.

Since the age of eleven, Queen of Spades flowed with the fire of ideas indicative of rhythm inundated with stanzas. She made her writing debut as a presenter and poet in the anthology *Soulful Branches: Words and Sounds.* Her other poetry works include *Reflections of Soul,* the *Eclectic* collection (Skin Edition & Beyond the Skin), the *Spaded Truths* collection (Themes and Proclamations and Life-O-

Suction), *Private Pain: Amidst These Ashes*, and *R.I.P.(E).: Random Inspirations on Paper: (E)ve-olution*.

Queen of Spades also collaborates in subjects she is passionate about. She provided works in the April 2014 poetry anthology *Words of Fire and Ice* by Durham Editing and E-books. In addition, she partnered with fellow author MJ Holman addressing the stigma of mental illness: *The Sea of Conscience* and *Waves to Light*.

Storytelling took the spotlight alongside poetry in Queen's literary evolution. She has written five independent short stories: "Taint on Religion", "Mr. Bradley's Garden", "When Summer Lingers", "Finding My Heart", and "Gossip Girls". Furthermore, she has participated in a number of short story compilations, such as *Continuous Drips*, the *Concordant Vibrancy* anthology series (Unity, Vitality, Lustrate, Inferno, Extancy), and the *Divergent Ink* collection (Crackles of the Heart, Pleasure Prints). She released her first short story collection *A Scribe's Sentiments* in 2019.

Some tout Queen of Spades is a Poet of the People. Others classify her as a Life Writer. The primary quality that remains consistent is her dedication to contemporary creativity while remaining true to herself.

Author Website:
   authorqueenofspades.com/
Facebook:
   facebook.com/authorqueenofspades
Twitter:
   @authorqspades